EPS Pocket Guide :

Emotional
Positioning
System

Funily *<8o)
Live Love Laugh Play Create!

Copyright © 2009 by Sterling & Sher Love / SS Love

Publisher Funily Inc *<8o) 2009 Funily. com

The authors of this book do not dispense medical or psychological advice or prescribe the use of any technique as a form of treament for physical, emotional or medical problems without the advice of a physician, either directly or indirectly. The intent of the authors is only to offer information of a general nature to help you in your quest for emotional and spiritual well-being. In the event you use any of the information in this book for yourself, which is your constitutional right, the authors and the publisher assume no responsibility for your actions.

Library of Congress Cataloging-in-Publication Data

Love, Sterling & Sher / SS LOVE
EPS Pocket Guide: Emotional Positioning System /
Sterling and Sher Love
   p. cm.
ISBN: 978-0-9825007-7-4   (trade pbk.)

Tradepaper ISBN 13: 978-0-9825007-7-4

EPS Pocket Guide :

Emotional
Positioning
System

Guide to Your Next BEST Feeling!

Authors & Artists :
Sterling & Sher Love

Fun :

Playful
   Enjoyment
   Amusement
LAUGHTER

EPS Pocket Guide :
Emotional Positioning System

About this Book :

A short, Fun, easy guide to help you to know what you're feeling right now and move you to the next best feeling with the ultimate goal of feeling Great Joy, Love, Appreciation, and the Freedom of Self Empowerment to choose exactly how and when you want to feel better in any given situation, time or place.

After all you want to feel Great!
You Deserve to feel Great! You are Great!
Life is ALL About Having FUN & Feeling GOOD!

Benefit: The more you use this book the better you'll feel, and the Better YOU Feel, WOO HOO! the BETTER YOU FEEL ... You get the idea!

Guide to Your Next BEST Feeling!

So let's get started...

EPS Simple Instructions :

1 Thumb through the pages and find the feeling definition that best describes how you feel right now. If it's close, or split between 2 feelings, choose the one that moves you in the direction you wish to go now.

2 Turn the page to shift to the next best feeling, recognize it and find the new improved feeling within yourself. Now FEEL IT... think about it, FOCUS on the New Feeling – and –

3 C O N G R A T U L A T E YourSelf for F e e l i n g B E T T E R !

4 Repeat as Necessary. Have FUN!

JOY :

Blissful
Enthusiastic
Exciting
Fun :-)

1

LOVE :

Incredibly
Strong Positive
Affection
of the Heart

2

BLISS :

Glowing
Pure Joy
Complete
Happiness

3

Appreciation :

Love
Gratitude
Recognition
Celebration

4

Freedom :

Relaxed
 Carefree
Powerful
Independent

5

Empowered :

Confident
Free
Fearless
Awesome!

6

Passion :

Burning
Intense Love
Affection
Desire

7

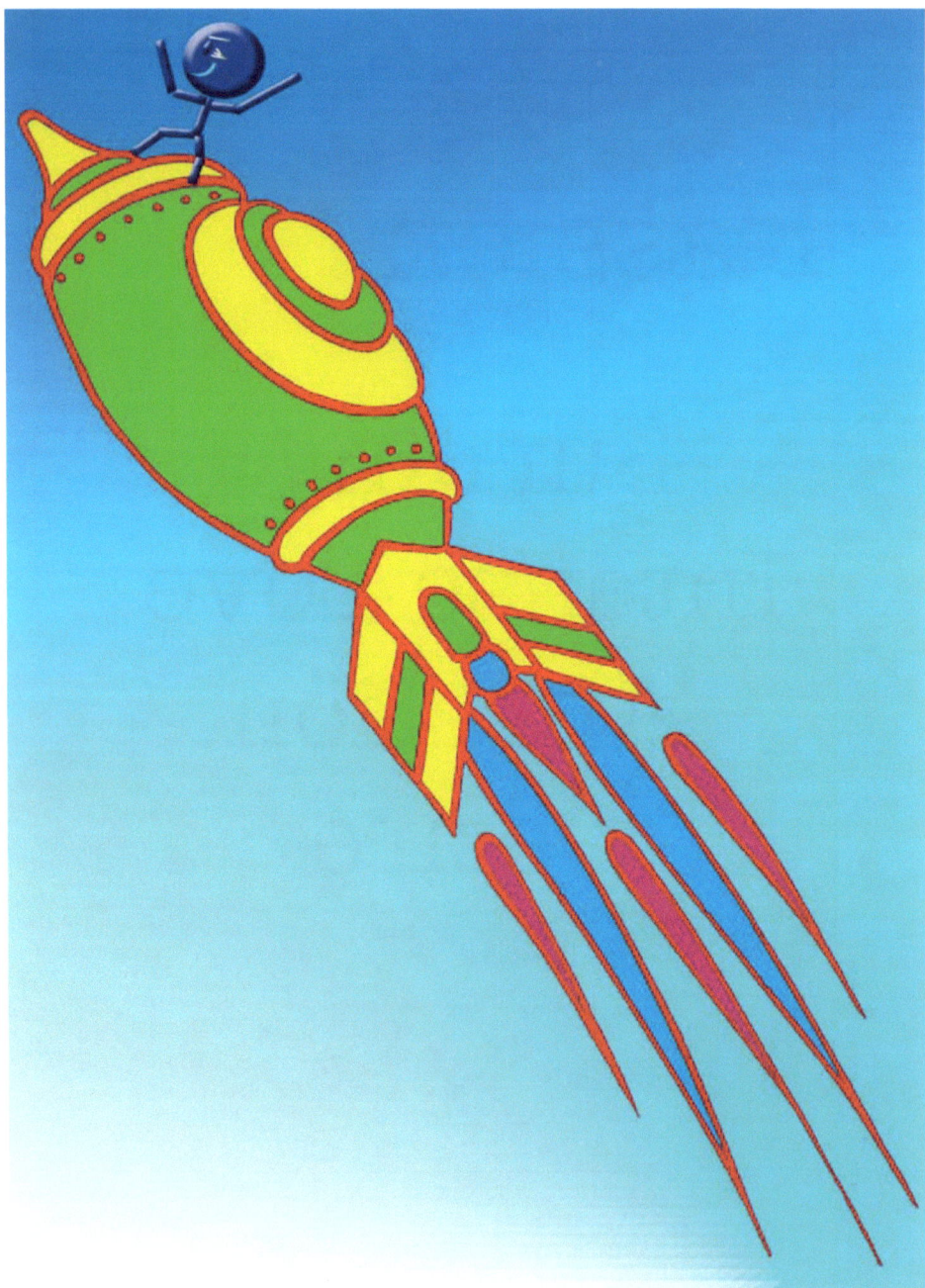

Enthusiasm :

Lively
Vibrating
Energetic
Inspiration

8

Eagerness :

Ready...
Set...
GO !
OH YEAH !

9

Happiness :

Being You
Enjoying Life
Pleasure
Laughter

10

Expectation :

Dream Big
Anticipate
Imagine
Receiving

11

Optimism :

Cheerful
Positive
Outlook
Insight

12

Hopeful :

Believe
Trust
Expect
Treasure

13

Content :

Happy with
Your Self
Your Life
Your Creations

14

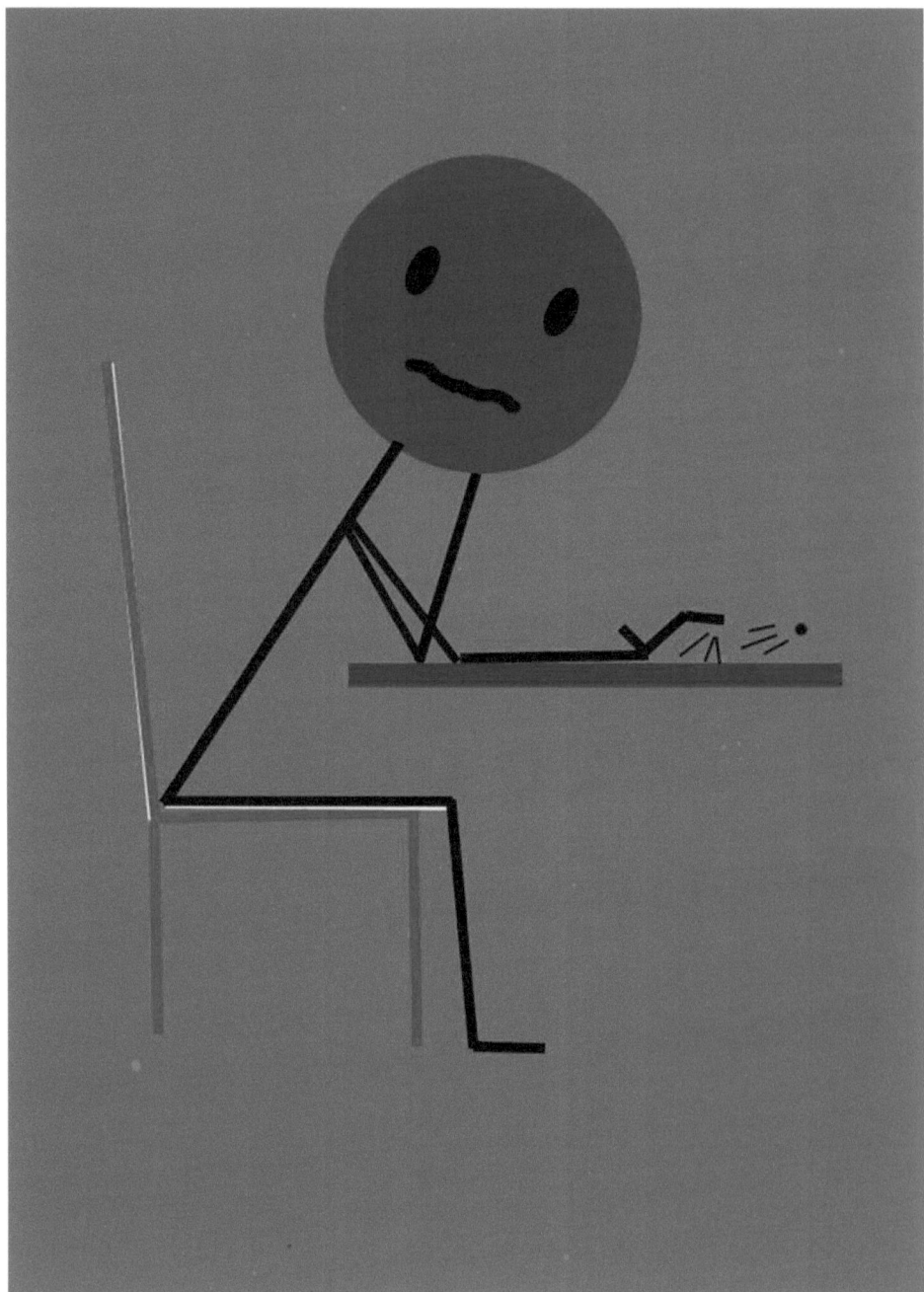

Bored :

Unenthusiastic
Uninterested
Uninspired
Uneventful

15

Impatience :

intolerant
restless
bothered
discontent

16

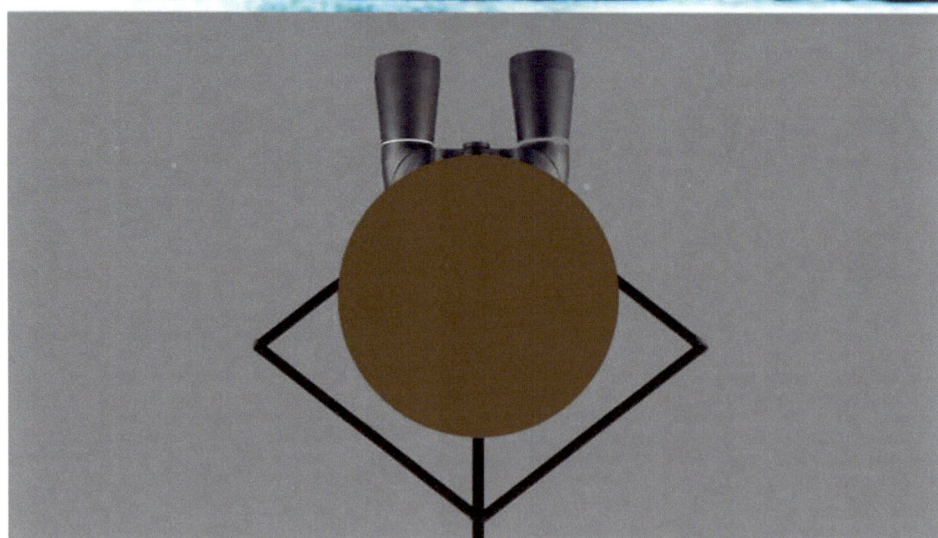

Pessimism :

doom and gloom
negative outlook
expecting things
to turn out badly

17

Frustration :

annoyance
dissatisfaction
unfulfilled
desires :-(

18

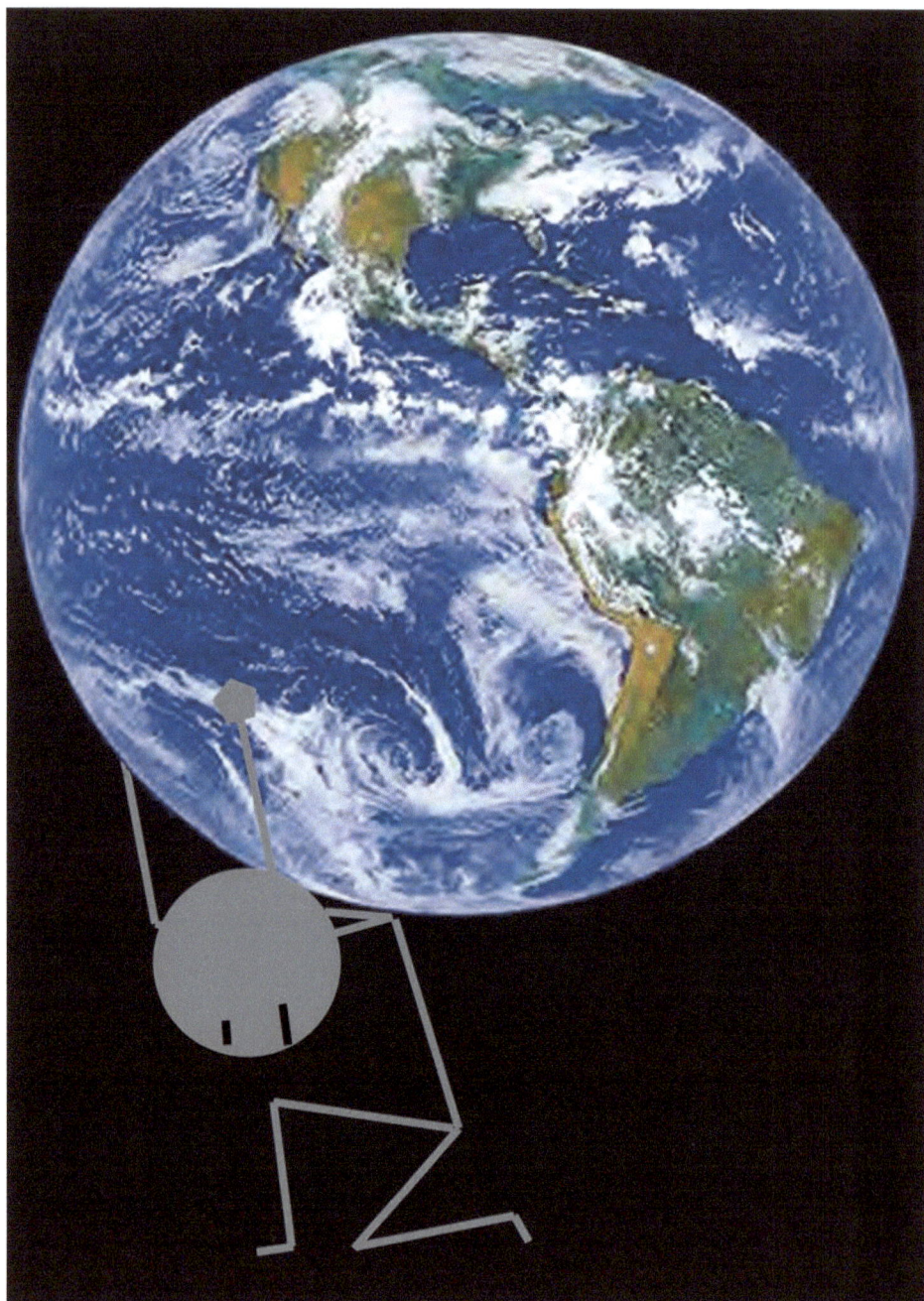

Overwhelmed :

depleted empty
exhausted
stressed
resistance

19

Doubt :

fear disbelief
uncertainty
lack confidence
distorted reality

20

Worry :

disturbed
peace of mind
mental torment
what if ?

21

Blame :

Not Taking Responsibility

criticism

accusations

22

Anger :

irritation
resentment
displeasure
hostility

23

Rage :

hysteria
    rampage
turmoil
fury frenzy

24

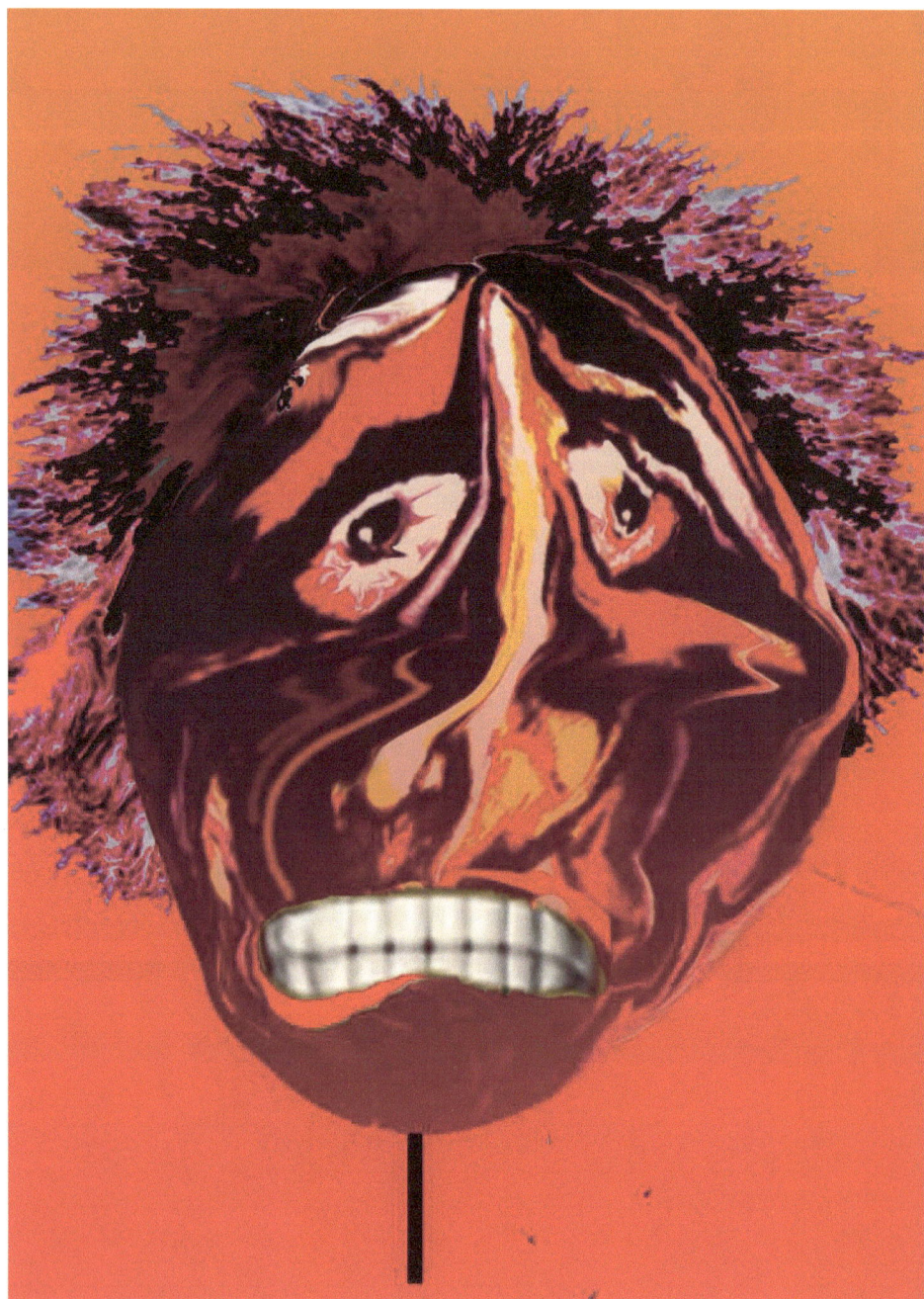

Anxiety :

uneasy creepy
vulnerable
insecure
fearing ???

25

Unworthy :

valueless
useless
underserving
low self esteem

26

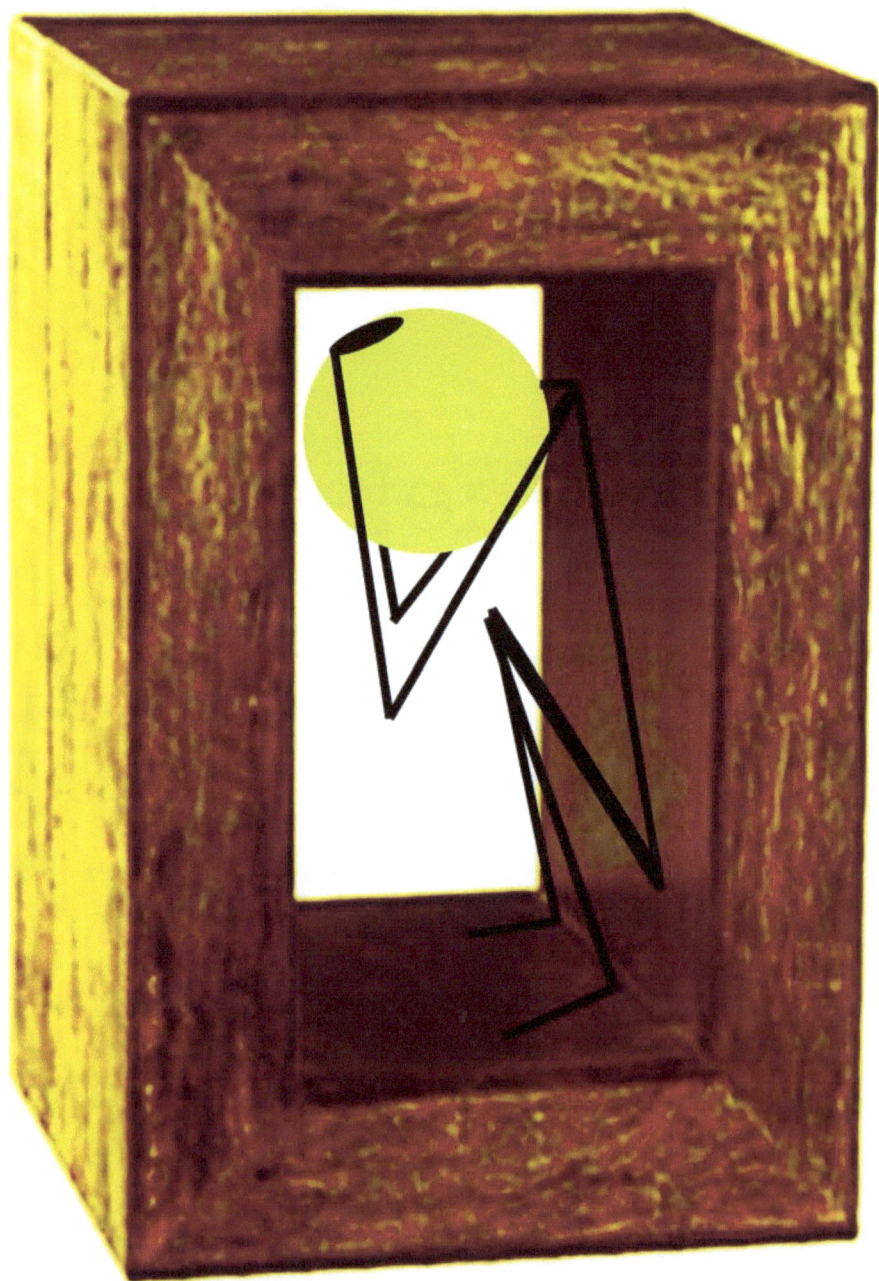

Fear :

apprehension
suspicion panic
False **E**vents
Appearing **R**eal

27

Grief :

intense sorrow
severe suffering
pain loss lack
agony

28

Depression :

sad gloomy
discouraged
down hearted
WOE is YOU!

29

Powerless :

helpless
lost all hope
weak
self denial

30

EPS 2 EYE

Expand Your Emotions :
COMING SOON !
EPSPocketGuide.com

Simple :

Relax

Easy

Focus

Flow

EPS Authors AfterWords :

Attitudes and moods are like vibrations that affect everything around us, especially self environmental impacts and benefits, every second of every day.

Our daily and long term lives are largely a creation of the emotions we feel moment to moment.

When You Feel Great You Know It!
Your feelings are like indicators on a roadmap.

With so many feelings and emotions available to create Your Present and Future Realities, it is important to **Recognize YOUR Feelings ARE Creating Your Life.**

You have absolute total control every moment. Consciously choose to think a new thought now to create an improved emotion and instantly feel better.

EPS can help you identify your emotions and serve as a guide to point you to your next best feeling.

Why do it? To have fun Fun FUN and feel great JOY.
EPS is not a "SECRET", YOU Have EPS Guidance Now.

USE IT. Shift your perspective and instantly change thoughts-beliefs-attitudes to see your improvement.

Just Flip the Pages!

Practice and See Improvement in Your Own Reality!

EPS Pocket Guide is an Easy Powerful Fun Tool You Can Use to Realize Your True Potential and Create A LIFE YOU LOVE TO LIVE and BE HAPPY NOW.

In any situation simply choose self alignment to create a more carefree fabulous life. By listening to your own inner guidance, you can experience life without all the drama and strife unconsciousness brings.

BENEFITS : Being Happy and Feeling Great Joy is the single most important thing you can do right now to improve the overall quality of your daily life, health and well being.

You know what feels good and what feels bad to you. Go the fun easy way or the hard way, it's up to you.

So if you don't like how you are currently feeling, look in the book to see where you are heading and figure out how to turn around to find an improved thought. Begin By Shifting Your Perspective.

HOW YOU FEEL IS ALWAYS YOUR CHOICE.
It's Really Simple, Position Yourself for FUN!
Allowing Your Own Happiness Feels Great!

Lighten Up and Let Your Own Feelings Guide You.

Say YES to What Feels Good to YOU. Focus on feeling really really really good great awesome fantastic!

It Is ALL About Recognizing if you are allowing good things to come? OR disallowing your own happiness?

FLIP the Pages for a **Humorous Look in the Mirror!** KNOW How in Alignment You Are With Your SELF.

The Benefits of Knowing Your Emotional Position and which Direction You Are Heading ARE Invaluable!

POWERFUL is when YOU Understand Your Emotions. AND Recognize How YOU are Feeling in the Moment.

WOW! What POWER! AIM FOCUS SCORE! FUN!

Mood Attitude Vibration Creation SELF Realization

Remember, YOU are ALWAYS in the Drivers Seat!

YOU have the Freedom to Chose How You Feel Next and you can continue to feel the same or change.

Your Life Can Be a Magical Mystery Fun Excursion OR ... miserable drama ... You choose which emotional rides you take, which experiences you make.

Resistance is Self Separation From Your Happiness!

Emotions can be sparked in an instant depending on your particular thought associations. Your experiences are personal and being viewed with your own unique filters and perceptions.

Perhaps you are feeling Overwhelmed by too much to do, Pessimistic you won't be able get it done, and Impatient because it isn't moving fast enough.

Blaming someone else for how you feel is sort of like exchanging Your Own Personal Freedom and Joy for Powerlessness essentially enslaving yourself. **OUCH!**

Disruptions to happiness can happen, when they do it is often difficult to access a good feeling emotion from a place of despair. It's sort of like driving out of a THICK FOG, before you can see everything more clearly again.

Blame... **if you let it** ... rampantly runs amuck ... and it can get you in some pretty sticky messes! You could have saved yourself the miserable trip.

Once You Consciously Know and Understand Your Own Feelings and **ACCEPT RESPONSIBILITY** for Your Emotions, it's Easy to Shift for Instant Self Improvement.

It is always your choice to accept responsibility or not.

CONGRATULATIONS!

As You View Your Own Emotions and SEE What IS Truly Happening, **You Can Easily Re-Empower Your SELF.**

The more you look for and see good in your life, and FOCUS on looking for what you want to see, the more joy, happiness and fun you will personally experience.

Emotions can help us understand our life positioning. Ask yourself if your current thought or belief is bringing you any pleasure to continue to think it?

You can choose any time in any situation to stay with your feelings or change your thought to feel more Optimistic, Happy or Appreciative.

At times we jump and spin all over the emotional chart! (feeling handfuls of emotions changing constantly)

Consciously Decide How You Want to Feel and Choose to Think a NEW Idea that will Create, Support, Produce and Inspire a New Emotion that Will Improve How You Feel.

Never loose your way again. By Choosing to Follow Your Own EPS Guidance System You Become Self Empowered and In True Control of Your Own Life.

Take the Next Right Step!

FLIP the EPS Guidance System Pages!

Use it, Play with it, Laugh, Have Fun and improve your life and relationships without being so serious.

"Get so fixated on what you want, that you drown out any vibration or reverberation that has anything to do with what you do not want." - Abraham - Hicks

This book is a compilation of art, ideas, knowledge and FUN! Our hope is that EPS will help others learn to live their lives in a state of Harmony, Bliss, Love and Joy!

EPS Pocket Guide is Enlightening Fun For All Ages.

Share it with your Lover, the Kids, share with the BT's (Be Tweens), the T's (Teens), the P's (Parents), and the GP's (Grand Parents), Friends, Coworkers & Strangers.

Keep Your EPS Pocket Guide Handy to Keep Feeling GREAT and Continue Being the BEST YOU EVERY DAY!

Your EPS Guidance is With YOU ALL THE TIME!

We Wish You The BEST... Easy FUN Happy Good Times!

Aloha, Love, Peace, Happiness & Appreciation!

Sher & Sterling Love

EPS Some Favorite Quotes :

If you change the way you look at things, the things you look at change. - AND - Freedom means you are unobstructed in living your life as you choose.
- Dr. Wayne Dyer

Be Happy, Practice Feeling Good! Don't give anyone else responsibility for the way you feel and then you love them all. The only reason you don't love them, is you're using them as your excuse to not feel good.
- Abraham-Hicks

The purpose of our lives is to be happy.
- Dalai Lama

Thoughts are things! And powerful things at that, when mixed with definiteness of purpose, and burning desire, can be translated into riches.
- Napoleon Hill

All You Need is Love.
Yoko Ono & John Lennon

What I know is, is that if you do work that you love, and the work fulfills you, the rest will come.
- Oprah Winfrey

We are responsible for everything in our lives.
- Rhonda Byrne

EPS More Favorite Quotes :

Change will not come if we wait for some other person or some other time. We are the ones we've been waiting for. We are the change that we seek.
- Barack Obama

Awareness without action is worthless. If you want more, you have to require more from yourself.
- Dr. Phil McGraw

Happiness is a continuation of happenings which are not resisted. Nothing is more important, more rich or more real than reconnecting with your bliss.
- Deepak Chopra

Happiness is the natural state of our being, I keep it foremost in my mind all day.
- Dr. Michael Beckwith

Your purpose is joy, you are joy. You are love, joy and freedom and clarity expressing. Pure Positive Energy - frolicking - eager -that's who you are.
- Abraham-Hicks

Peace and Love. Peace and Love. Choose Love.
- Ringo Starr

Thoughts Become Things. Choose Good Ones!
- Mike Dooley

Authors, Artists, Creators :
Sterling & Sher Love aka SS LOVE

Together we live life adventurously pursuing our fun artistic passions expanding in various enriching ways.

Through our love and the practice and applications of universal laws and principles, we have created an amazingly wonderful life where we live, love, laugh, play and create together every day! Life is FUN!

The quotes are our love acknowledgements for a mere few of the insightful wonderful people who have so generously touched all our lives by being living proof of the powerful nature of conscious creation!

We appreciate this opportunity to share a wealth of valuable insights with you in a FUN filled way and hope you enjoy flipping the pages as much as we enjoyed creating them.

This publishing of our first wisdom filled art book is the beginning of more Fun Exciting things to come!

For More Information, Fun and Gifts Visit Our
WEBSITE: EPSPocketGuide.com

About the Artists :
Sterling & Sher Love aka SS LOVE

**To View Our Wildly Fabulous Leading Edge ART
Paintings and Other ART Projects Visit Our**

WEBSITE: SSLoveART.com

As Fine Contemporay Abstract Artists We Create
Unique Leading Edge Paintings and ART Projects.

Exhibiting Fabulous Colorful Bold Exotic Love Art

LOVE
Museum of Modern Art

LoveMoMA.org

A Portion of Our Proceeds Benefit

LOVE ART FOUNDATION 501c3
LoveArtFoundation.org

www.ingramcontent.com/pod-product-compliance
Lightning Source LLC
Chambersburg PA
CBHW041530090426

42738CB00035B/17